WHAT TO DO WHEN NO ONE ELSE ENCOURAGES YOU

40 DAYS OF ENCOURAGEMENT FOR YOUR MIND, HEART, & SOUL

Kathryn Adams

Life is beautiful, challenging, hard, and sometimes overwhelmingly surprising. In times like these when your back is against the wall and your head hangs low you must find a way to encourage yourself. Discouragement isn't prejudice, it's not like a child that's a picky eater; discouragement will seek out to come face to face with anyone regardless of your status, stature, or ethnicity. If you have a goal, a dream, a positive thought to wake up and enjoy oxygen you must fight off discouragement. It dresses up in the form of bad news, let downs, and disappointments. Encouraging people, gifts, signs, and digital messages are all a blessing. Yet, if no one takes the time to invest that positive pour of hope into your cup you must find a way to drink from the Living Waters himself. I am talking about encouraging yourself in the Lord. Encouraging yourself from the word of God daily. Self-encouragement is investment in your spirit. It's mandatory and can be contagious in you, through you, and upon you. It's important for us to be filled and constantly fill ourselves with God's word. There are times when you will be in place of ultimate attack but that's the very place to take step one of encouraging you. Encouragement is defined as the action of giving someone support, confidence, or hope. Everyone that was great in the bible and in history that you have read about, heard, and seen have fought off discouragement. Some of our greatest inventors who have change the course of how we do everyday life had to find a way to overcome obstacles and several challenges. In the face of ridicule, discouragement, and adversity they found a way. God is our Way, he is our Rock, he is our Living Waters and Bread of Life. We can't do anything without him, so I encourage you to receive encouragement from him. Sometimes when we're going through people can be lost with words as much as they talk; and they could genuinely care but don't know how to express it in words. I found this happening to me since I was the person that a lot of family and friends often came to during their hard times. Don't be angry or offended, God understands you and he cares for you during your quietness, sadness, depression, loneliness, and feeling of abandonment. He is right there with you. In this devotional book I want to encourage you through scriptures that have encouraged me. I often find myself praying them out loud in prayer and even in that I found that encouragement begins to flow. It's important for you to be encouraged because God cares about your spirit, soul, and body. Lift your head and know that Jesus loves you and is on your side in the midst of it all. So, I encourage you to encourage yourself in the Lord and his wonderful word.

CONTENTS

Day 1 To Remember That We Are Loved-pg5

Day 2 He Thinks of Me-pg5

Day 3 To Trust Who I Don't See-pg6

Day 4 Peace Over-pg6

Day 5 Fixed-pg7

Day 6 Powerful Faith-pg7

Day 7 On Purpose Praise-pg8

Day 8 Mercies & Compassions-pg9

Day 9 A Different Kind of Happy-pg9

Day 10 Deliverance, Deliverance, Deliverance! -pg10

Day 11 Hard After Thee-pg11

Day 12 Truth Confessed-pg11

Day 13 Prayer Benefits-12

Day 14 Preservation in My dedication-pg12

Day 15 God and Shield-pg13

Day 16 This Commandment-pg13

Day 17 Training Camp-pg14

Day 18 What He Gave-pg14

Day 19 He Will-pg15

Day 20 Pre-Praise-pg15

Day 21 Solution for an Anxious Heart-pg16

Day 22 A Walk Begins-pg16

Day 23 The Forgiveness Circle-pg17

Day 24 Wrong Perception-pg17

Day 25 Did You Know?-pg18

Day 26 Hand and Hand-pg18

Day 27 The Cross-pg19

Day 28 Spiritual Inventory-pg19

Day 29 The Order-pg20

Day 30 Answers to Your Questions-pg20

Day 31 Help Is Here-pg21

Day 32 Delight Yourself-pg22

Day 33 Set Apart-pg22

Day 34 He Is-pg23

Day 35 I Dare You to Sing-pg23

Day 36 Discern the Cry-pg24

Day 37 Ages and Stages-pg24

Day 38 Wash Me Lord-pg25

Day 39 You Are-pg25

Day 40 Find A Way-pg26

Journal & Reflection-pg27

Day 01

1 John 4:19 We love him, because he first loved us.

To Remember That We Are Loved

My flaws sometimes deceive me, mistakes make me feel not so great, my faith it undergirds me to remind me that I'm far from hate, and brings me rest and comfort from above, I'm reminded that I'm loved.

Encouragement: God Loves You.

I'm telling you he simply does. His love is so expensive and yet he charges us nothing, it costs him everything just to get to you and me. I encourage you today, believe it receive it, walk in it, breathe in and out and know that you are loved.

Day 02

Jeremiah 29:11 For I know the thoughts that I think toward you, saith the LORD, thoughts of peace, and not of evil, to give you an expected end.

He Thinks of Me

He thinks of me. Spirit and dust, that's what I am and he thinks of me. Good thoughts and crazy ways of mine, but he thinks of me. When I'm not super spiritual and even wrong he thinks of me. He's always thinking, doing, and showing me his good ways, loving ways, forgiving ways. Makes me want to think of him more and more. I love the way he thinks about me.

Encouragement: Thinking about him having you on his mind is encouraging.

Let the Lord be your meditation, take this day to meditate on him. Get rid of the overwhelming, depressing, negative, down thoughts and fill your mind with Him. Put the word of God on your desktop, phone, tablet, in your ears and before your eyes. Refresh your spirit invest in your encouragement.

Day 03

Proverbs 3:5, 6 Trust in the LORD with all thine heart; and lean not unto thine own understanding. In all thy ways acknowledge him, and he shall direct thy paths.

To Trust Who I Don't See

I walk by faith I walk in you. I live by faith that's what I do. You are the compass in my soul, I'm led by you that's what I know. I trust your love and guiding hand, you are the rock, I am the sand. I bow my knees humbly and pray, I trust you Lord you are the way. Some may doubt and not believe but I trust in you who I don't see.

Encouragement: We are faith walkers.

There were times I trusted in me, in money, in men and women; setting my faith in things and people that could crumble, fall apart, and die. I made a solid decision one day to trust him with all of my heart. Choose to trust God ask him to help you, lead you, and guide you in whatever you need help in and with. God will instruct you on what to when you don't lean to your own understanding.

Day 04

Psalm 119:165 Great peace have they which love thy law: and nothing shall offend them.

Peace Over

Peace over and over again, more peace than before. I gave chaos the door and let in peace in. Peace over and over again, more than before. I kicked confusion out and sent away doubt. I fell in love with the Word, haven't you heard? I have a real relationship with the word. I'm embracing peace over and over again. Peace has a name it is the Lord, and Jesus is my friend.

Encouragement: Jesus is King and Prince. He is your Prince of Peace, his kingdom rules overall.

You know it's nothing like peace. I mean real peace from the inside out. Quiet places don't necessarily guarantee peacefulness. Let the King of Kings rule and sit on the throne of your heart and peace will remain regardless of what storms you're in or what storms are trying to enter you.

Day 05

Psalm 57:7 My heart is fixed, O God, my heart is fixed: I will sing and give praise.

Fixed

He fixed me when I was broken, he healed me when I was sick. He lifted me up when I was down. He gave me joy when I was sad, lost in this world and he found me. Stopped the clutches of death and all adversaries around me. Confronted me about my sinful ways and I yield my all and give God the praise.

Encouragement: A set heart to praise God is beautiful.

Fixed is defined as fastened securely in position. When you decide no matter what you're going to praise God victory is always present. Daily life is unpredictable, but God is faithful and he never changes nor fails, so praise him because he's worthy to be praised.

Day 06

1 John 5:4 For whatsoever is born of God overcometh the world: and this is the victory that overcometh the world, *even* our faith.

Powerful Faith

Powerful faith, invisible faith, wonderful faith that comes from God. He is the word and when it is heard, those that are born, are encouraged, and warned to keep their faith. Such an invisible thing, yet the thief comes to steal it from hearts that won't allow-it to take root. But overcomers they know with their faith they grow and go forward in victory.

Encouragement: Being born again is a beautiful thing.

To overcome the world can only be done in God. It is so much pulling, tugging, and calling us away from him daily. From the time we awake until we lay down all sorts of worldly things are trying to seduce us out of our faith. Keep your faith it's a weapon.

Day 07

Psalm 119:164 Seven times a day do I praise thee because of thy righteous judgments.

On Purpose Praise

This was done on purpose, I opened my eyes and praised you. My feet touched the floor and I praise you, I stretched and yarn and begin to praise you again. Seven praises are a good start but when I think of what you've did in my heart, I have to go for number eight. Everything I am, have and will become is all because of you. All my strength to be successful comes from you, the food I eat that you allowed me to buy, chew and swallow comes from you. On Purpose I praise you because you are so good to me.

Encouragement: Make praise a good habit. Do it on purpose.

Everything that we have in our life is important and we owe God the praise because without him we could do nothing. From the sinner to the saint, it's because of him that we are even alive. I believe that's worth taking the time right now to praise God. Praise shifts the atmosphere it uplifts you to a place of gratefulness. Praise ushers you into the presence of God immediately and reminds you of who holds the power to change whatever is affecting us in life. Release a praise in a song or just an attitude of gratitude to God. He inhabits our praises, and he enjoys our presence in his

Day 08

Lamentations 3:22-23 It is of the LORD'S mercies that we are not consumed, because his compassions fail not. They are new every morning: great is thy faithfulness.

Mercies & Compassions

To get something we didn't deserve, to receive something that he gives, it was all him, it was all him. No one is merciful like the Lord nor will ever be, no one is compassionate like God, the God who loves me. I am not consumed by him nor doomed by him because his compassions they don't fail. He never runs dry, empty, out or low; he's God and it's all him. To get something we didn't deserve, to receive something that he gives, and they are new every morning.

Encouragement: Acknowledging God's mercies and compassions in your life is important.

When we were sinners, completely separated from him, doing everything that we wanted to his love extended to us through Jesus. Everyday is a gift that he has given us, every breath is a blessing from him. Remember him and don't forget about his goodness he has shown to you daily.

Day 09

Proverbs 16:20 He that handleth a matter wisely shall find good: and whoso trusteth in the LORD, happy is he.

A Different Kind of Happy

I have a different kind of happy. I'm happy if it turns out good or not. I'm happy if it's cold or hot. I'm happy when it rains and pours; I'm happy for shut and open doors. When trouble comes and decisions must be made; I pray to God and humbly adhere to his ways. Why? Because I have a different kind of happy.

Encouragement: Wisdom from God and trust in God are connected.

When I'm going through things and I find myself becoming uneasy, discontent, and unhappy I back track my thoughts. Every time I've handle a matter wisely, I was resting and trusting in God, and every time I didn't the outcome wasn't good. Ask God for wisdom, trust in him and you will have a different kind of happy.

Day 10

Psalm 116:8 For thou hast delivered my soul from death, mine eyes from tears, and my feet from falling.

Deliverance, Deliverance, Deliverance!

God delivered me! I said, "God delivered me!" My soul was in trouble, looking death in the eyes with no escape, no place to hide, no place to run. My eyes were filled with water, heart was in pain, mind mourn the thought of going on. My feet were in a fallen place where they shouldn't have been. But God in his loving kindness, in his merciful ways delivered me and now I give him the glory.

Encouragement: Getting delivered, being delivered, and staying delivered is mandatory.

Spiritual freedom is highly appreciated by those who were bound. Remembering God's deliverance that took place in your life is encouraging. His power is greater than all. Staying delivered from whatever had you in chains is a purposeful decision made daily. Compromising your liberty to fit in is not worth giving up the victory God has given you through Jesus Christ. Deliverance from bondages and chains is what Christ died and rose for: to destroy the works of the devil so that we could be eternally free. That freedom, our freedom the freedom for the entire world cost him everything. Live in it, walk in it, and be it; above all things continue to look to him for strength and deliverance.

Day 11

Psalm 63:8 My soul followeth hard after thee: thy right hand upholdeth me.

Hard After Thee

They say, "You're too faithful". I say, "I'm following hard after God". They say, "You're too loving". I say, "I'm following hard after God." They say, "You're too focused". I say, "I'm following hard after God". Hard after the God who redeemed me. Hard after the God who purified my heart. Hard after the God who healed me. Hard after the God who took away the darkness in my life. I don't care what they say at all, I only know that I'm going hard after God.

Encouragement: Don't let anyone discourage you from going hard after God.

It's okay to be grateful, unashamed, boldly in love with God Go after God with your whole heart and let nothing and no one stop you.

Day 12

Psalm 145:18 The Lord is nigh unto all them that call upon him, to all that call upon him in truth.

Truth Confessed

The reality of the call was this, I had to confess in truth, and I had to confess the truth. This time I came serious, prepared, and humbled before God. This time I came open with no deceptive games in my heart. This time I came sincerely, in truth, confessed. This time when I got up from praying, I had real soul rest.

Encouragement: Being close to the Lord for real is more important than anything else in the world. Call upon him every day. Everyday call upon God.

Being real with yourself and God makes the deliverance that you need to take place more effectively. We don't have to hide anything from him, the truth is we can't anyway. If you call upon him in truth you will see his power move in your life.

Day 13

Psalm 145:19 He will fulfil the desire of them that fear him: he also will hear their cry, and will save them.

Prayer Benefits

When I cry, when I pray, tears streaming down while on my knees and on my face; he hears me, and I can't quit. I go to him because I have prayer benefits. My desire is fulfilled, prayer heard, and I am saved. God calms the storms and makes my enemies behave. Rather joy or sorrow, pain or pleasure, when I open my mouth, I have access to heaven. He hears me and I can't quit, I go to him because I have prayer benefits.

Encouragement: The scriptures are guaranteed promises to you and for you.

Crying out to God is not a disadvantage it is an advantage, a privilege, and covenant access that Christ gave us. We belong to him. He is our God, powerful and mighty; use your benefits.

Day 14

Psalm 145:20 The Lord preserveth all them that love him: but all the wicked will he destroy.

Preservation In My dedication

I'm dedicated and committed to God. He has my eyes, soul, heart, and yes, my body too. The relationship originated in his heart towards me. Why wouldn't I be dedicated to him? His love is genuine and everlasting. His love covered me and calmed me. He wrapped his loving arms around me in this cold wicked place. He gave me strength to run this race, he gave me truth to walk by faith. I'm preserved because I love him, and he loves me too.

Encouragement: Love God simply love him.

It's important for you to love God and to be good to him. This relationship goes both ways. Ask him to show you how to love him, and serve him better more and more.

Day 15

Proverbs 30:5 Every word of God is pure: he is a shield unto them that put their trust in him.

God and Shield

He is one and both for me. God is God and Shield. He's my peace and victory. When fiery darts are launched and traps are set, he's God who keeps my feet out of the net. He is both for me. God is God and Shield.

Encouragement: The war never stops therefore always know that you will need God for ever.

Knowing God's word is knowing him. It goes beyond scriptural memorization. Trusting God at his word is trusting in him. Let God be both for you in your life concerning everything.

Day 16

Joshua 1:9 Have not I commanded thee? Be strong and of a good courage; be not afraid, neither be thou dismayed: for the LORD thy God is with thee whithersoever thou goest.

This Commandment

This commandment is not the ten, yet important deep within. This commandment doesn't scream and shout, but this commandment casts out fear and doubt. This commandment encourages you to fight. This commandment put your enemies to flight. Be strong and of a good courage.

Encouragement: Strength and courage comes from God.

Being in his presence privately and corporately makes the difference. You have to know that you can only make it with the strength, courage, and help of God. He's with you never leaving. God is un-moveable, impenetrable, eternal, solid foundation.

Day 17

Psalm 144:1 Blessed be the LORD my strength which teacheth my hands to war, and my fingers to fight:

Training Camp

The camp where soldiers are made, the camp where soldiers are trained is the camp God has me in. Young David killing his lion and the bear, slaying Goliath without a care. Gideon with his 300 on the battle scene, and Samson killing thousands of Philistines-came through this place. While Joshua slayed his foes and put his feet on their necks to let them all know that God is King. This is the training ground where victors stand, the king and captain of this army is God and not man.

Encouragement: Know that you are called to be a good soldier.

You are in the army of God. The weapons are the word of God and prayer. Training camp is mandatory; fear not just remember God is king and captain.

Day 18

2 Timothy 1:7 For God hath not given us the spirit of fear; but of power, and of love, and of a sound mind.

What He Gave

What he gave you is power to tread over. What he gave you is love that is fervent.

What he gave you is a sound mind to think, understand, and to know. All that other stuff cast it down, cast it out, and cast it away because that's not what he gave you!

Encouragement: You have the tools, and the weapons so use them boldly.

In order to know what he hasn't given you; you must know what he has given you. It is all written in your bible. Read it. Know it.

Day 19

Isaiah 50:7 For the Lord God will help me; therefore shall I not be confounded: therefore have I set my face like a flint, and I know that I shall not be ashamed.

He Will

He will show up, yes, he will. He will show out, yes, he will. He will shower down upon me; he will rise up within me. He will provide for me as he has done so many times before. He will block and close every counterfeit door. He will because he's God and there's nothing and no one can do about it.

Encouragement: God is willing to help you because he loves you.

When you know above all knowing that God will do what he will in your life, nothing will move you. It's guaranteed opposition will come but through it all even until the end you must know that you will not be ashamed or left to shame.

Day 20

1Corinthians 15:57 But thanks be to God, which giveth us the victory through our Lord Jesus Christ.

Pre-Praise

Before it happens, before it manifests in plain sight, before I lay my hands on it; thank you Lord for victory. I praise you here. I praise you now. I praise you before I even ask. I praise you while I wait, I praise you when it comes. For now, I'll say, "Thank you for hearing me!".

Encouragement: You have victory right now.

Sometimes victory don't feel, see, or look like victory; but you have victory. Yes, here today, right now. God gets the glory because we have victory through Jesus.

Day 21

Philippians 4:6 Be careful for nothing; but in every thing by prayer and supplication with thanksgiving let your requests be made known unto God.

Solution For an Anxious Heart

When my heart begins to speak anxious things to me, I turned my concerns to God in prayer for the Lord will surely meet me there. When my heart tries to complain about things that I can't change, I lift my head to the sky and look to him whom I don't deny. When my heart tried to deceive me in siding with my enemies, I say out loud, "Greater is he who is within me". The conclusion to this solution is prayer to God from the start, that's my solution for an anxious heart.

Encouragement: God is greater than your heart, worry not take your heart before God.

God's presence is our calm in the storm and when there's no storm raging at all. When your heart tries to out talk your faith, take your heart to the creator, and see how your thoughts will shift, change, and line up in peace.

Day 22

Colossians 1:10 That ye might walk worthy of the Lord unto all pleasing, being fruitful in every good work, and increasing in the knowledge of God;

A Walk Begins

A walk begins with one step and then another. A worthy walk begins one day at a time, and then you a dd another. Pleasing the Lord begins with one choice of his over your own pleasure, one day at a time. So, walk. Let us begin, take the first step.

Encouragement: Walk worthy to please the Lord in every way.

It's an honor to walk in the love of God, truth of God, and the fear of God. Pleasing the Lord is not hard because his commandments are not grievous to us. We are to be productive spiritually in good works, as well as increasing in knowing him. This decision must be intentional because compromising is so easy to do.

Day 23

Colossians 3:13 Forbearing one another, and forgiving one another, if any man have a quarrel against any: even as Christ forgave you, so also do ye.

The Forgiveness Circle

It all depends what I extend to keep the circle round; for if I be fake make no mistake my sins shall surely be found. God has forgiven me and continues on as I forgive you and forgive myself; but if I be fake, hide harm and hate, this I can't surely get around. I must leave my gift, go get it straight and be fully reconciled. If I be forgiving, I'll be forgiven and that's what keeps the circle round.

Encouragement: Relationship with God commands you to forgive because it's love and liberty for everyone.

Forgiveness is a blessing for real, we receive freedom. Free up someone else and yourself so that you can enjoy God and each other. Christ set a high standard of love, but he knew we could reach it through him.

Day 24

1Thessalonians 5:9 For God hath not appointed us to wrath, but to obtain salvation by our Lord Jesus Christ,

Wrong Perception

He is not the abuser nor the accuser. He's not waiting for us to slip, trip, or flip to get us good. He knew we would. He is not magnifying my every little mistake to sentence me to eternal doom. You have the wrong perception of God. He is my escape; it was his idea to be the Way for me. He adores me, and you, and died for us all. He is the Deliverer, our Deliverance, our Eternal Salvation.

Encouragement: Knowing him intimately makes serving him easy. Even in the midst of afflictions you know it's worth it.

Some people serve God from a slave mentality. We honor and deeply reverence him because he loves us so. We draw close to him in this salvation he has given us.

Day 25

Hebrews 13:1 Let brotherly love continue.

Did You Know?

Did you know that you have family in heaven and in earth? Did you know that all of us that are washed and redeemed in Jesus' blood are family? We are united in the faith all connected by God's love. We must, "Let brotherly love continue". This is the identification card that the world sees and know that we're disciples of the Lord.

Encouragement: Our ultimate example of love in heaven and in earth is Jesus.

Love is active, kind, selfless. All of this is to be given and allowed freely to our brothers and sisters in Christ. Let it flow through you, let it continue.

Day 26

1 John 4:20 If a man say, I love God, and hateth his brother, he is a liar: for he that loveth not his brother whom he hath seen, how can he love God whom he hath not seen?

Hand and Hand

Loving and knowing goes hand and hand. I can't love God and hate my fellow man. I haven't seen God but I see my family in Christ. I can't hate them and proclaim Christ to be in my life. Loving and knowing goes hand and hand. I can't love God and hate my fellow man.

Encouragement: 1 John 4:8 He that loveth not knoweth not God; for God is love.

Loving God is expressed in truth from the heart first and lived out in our lives. Our love for him and our brothers and sisters in Christ will be tested and tried. Remember, love never fails, love covers, love is patient and kind. God is love.

Day 27

1 Peter 4:16 Yet if any man suffer as a Christian, let him not be ashamed; but let him glorify God on this behalf.

The Cross

It's jewelry to some, beautifully, shining gold or silver; whatever you like. It's wood for some, standing tall and bold in a church yard, concrete in cemeteries, all over the world. It was suffering for Christ for sins he didn't commit. For accusations that rightfully belonged to us. Whatever your cross may be Christian, endure it, don't be ashamed of it, rejoice in it to the glory of God.

Encouragement: Luke 14:27 And whosoever doth not bear his cross, and come after me, cannot be my disciple.

I encourage you to take up your cross. It's a part of God's plan as well. Though it seems like a discouragement it isn't. Your suffering reminds you that you don't identify with the world.

Day 28

James 1:21, 22 Wherefore lay apart all filthiness and superfluity of naughtiness, and receive with meekness the engrafted word, which is able to save your souls. But be ye doers of the word, and not hearers only, deceiving your own selves.

Spiritual Inventory

What's needed? What has to go? What's stagnant with no spiritual flow? What needs to be refreshed? What needs to be refilled? What have I lost? What needs to be healed? I think it's only right to know what I need when I'm requesting help: so, I take this time to do spiritual inventory of myself.

Encouragement: Some things must be laid down and done away with in order to be able to run this race.

Hearing and not doing is a spiritual injustice to yourself. Hear the truth and do the truth. Hear the truth and live the truth. Don't be self-deceived, and especially by people you must do the word of God.

Day 29

James 4:7 Submit yourselves therefore to God. Resist the devil, and he will flee from you.

The Order

The order can not be broken. No special favors in this, it only works according to what is written. Submission is always first, there's power in the order. Submission is always first, there's victory in the order. Submission is always first, there's peace in the order. The order can't be broken.

Encouragement: Victory over anything always begin with submitting everything and all of you to God.

Be an empowered believer by being an obedient one. There's no resistance against the devil when you're not submitted to God.

Day 30

Ephesians 5:17 Wherefore be ye not unwise, but understanding what the will of the Lord is.

Answers To Your Questions

The "What's, how's, and whys", are in his will. The answers to your questions are in his word. His will is his word. Your answers are not far away as you suppose. Just take the time to know that you must take the time to seek the God of your salvation.

Encouragement: Christians can access God's wisdom and receive understanding of what his will is by getting into the word.

The word is Spirit and Life. The more time that you spend with God more clarity will be given to you concerning his will.

Day 31

John 14:26 But the Comforter, which is the Holy Ghost, whom the Father will send in my name, he shall teach you all things, and bring all things to

your remembrance, whatsoever I have said unto you.

Help Is Here

Before he left, he told us of another. Another who would stay with us greater than father and mother. The other who would be in us, being a present help always for us. He is the Comforter. Help is here. He has a plan. He is our help, he understands. So let him teach and guide you in truth, listen to the Comforter and let him do what he does; help and comfort every one of us.

Encouragement: You are not alone, abandoned, nor forsaken, the Comforter is here with you.

Read, study, and meditate on the scriptures about the Holy Spirit. The Lord specifically sent him here to help us. He will teach you and guide you into all truth, as well as bring Jesus' word back to your mind. Yielding your will is up to how much he can help you. He will not force you to do anything you have to have a willing and an obedient heart to be led by him in all things.

Day 32

Psalm 1:2 But his delight is in the law of the Lord; and in his law doth he meditate day and night.

Delight Yourself

Delight yourself in God's word, there's great reward. He has plenty laid up for you all in store. When you go to the throne make your request known, remind him of his covenant, and daily how you are loving it. Meditate in the scripture day and night, let them lead the way and be your light. Be diligent in your search, specific in your prayers, worry about nothing, casting all of your cares.

Encouragement: Delighting in God's word helps you make better decisions because of the wisdom and power that comes from the scriptures.

Everyone who meditated and diligently went after God always came out victorious and promoted in the face of their enemies. He did for them and he will do it for you.

Day 33

Psalm 4:3 But know that the Lord hath set apart him that is godly for himself: the Lord will hear when I call unto him.

Set Apart

You couldn't blend in with the world if you tried. God has his hands and eyes upon you. You couldn't stay in a low place and be content because God has his hands and eyes upon you. You're a godly person, handpicked on purpose, set apart for God himself. You are loved, anointed, special, and chosen; know it.

Encouragement: It's good to be set apart for God that means you're in relationship with him. He knows your voice and name.

God from the beginning made man to spend time with him. He loves us so much the enemy can't stand it. Who can overthrow God? No one can overthrow God be thankful you're set apart; it's an honor.

Day 34

Psalm 18:1,2 I will love thee, O Lord, my strength. The Lord is my rock, and my fortress, and my deliverer; my God, my strength, in whom I will trust; my buckler, and the horn of my salvation, and my high tower.

He Is

Whatever I need, he is. Whatever I need, he is. I Am that I Am is my God. A shelter, bread, water, a shield, a hiding place, a sword, whatever I need, he is.

Wherever I'm at he's there. On the mountain, in the valley. In peace, in war; wherever I'm at he's there.

Encouragement: Psalm 18:3 I will call upon the LORD, who is worthy to be praised: so, shall I be saved from mine enemies.

God is our saving strength. We can run to him, hide in him, cry to him, and he's everything and more all at the same time.

Day 35

Psalm 28:7 The LORD is my strength and my shield; my heart trusted in him, and I am helped: therefore my heart greatly rejoiceth; and with my song will I praise him.

I Dare You to Sing

I dare you to sing in tune and out. I dare you to rejoice so thunderously with a song that you shock your enemies. I dare you to rejoice from the depths of your heart. Let the praise flow like a wild river out of you. I dare you to.

Encouragement: The cute praise is played out. Give God the radical praise due to him.

When God delivers you there is no keeping quiet, praise is comely for the upright. It's necessary. It expresses thanks beyond a thought, it moves through your entire being. I dare you to praise God.

Day 36

Psalm 34:17 The righteous cry, and the LORD heareth, and delivereth them out of all their troubles.

Discern The Cry

The Lord can discern the cry. He speaks silence, he speaks tears, he speaks emotional sighs of frustration. He speaks the language of all men and he hears. His ears are open, he knows what you're crying out to him about and he will deliver you.

Encouragement: Keep crying out to God. Keep crying out until he brings you out.

Blind Bartimaeus got his sight. The people tried to quiet him, but he kept crying out until Jesus stopped and turned. Be encouraged, the Lord he hears your cry and is turning things around for you

Day 37

Psalm 37:25 I have been young, and now am old; yet have I not seen the righteous forsaken, nor his seed begging bread.

Ages and Stages

Ages and stages don't change the provision of God. He is from everlasting to everlasting. He is the same yesterday, today, and forever. Ages and stages don't change the provision of God. He's water in the desert and bread in the wilderness. Ages and stages don't change the provision of God. He is a cloud by day and fire by night. Whatever age or stage you're in God is God and he's more than enough.

Encouragement: God will never leave you. Your youth and gray hairs is a common thing to him even if it's shocking to you.

Day 38

Psalm 51:2 Wash me throughly from mine iniquity, and cleanse me from my sin.

Wash Me Lord

The sinner requested to be washed, the self-righteous saints laughed. The sinner took the plunge in the bloody bath. When the sinner came up clean, he had become a saint, the hypocrites they played and ignored the preacher's word. But the sinner who became a saint received the word he heard-and got washed

Encouragement: Repentance daily is good for the soul.

Daily we need to go before the Lord and let him search our hearts of anything that is offensive. We don't want to be self-righteous, having our own righteousness or hypocrites. Let the water of the word of God wash your heart and mind daily.

Day 39

Psalm 91:11 For he shall give his angels charge over thee, to keep thee in all thy ways.

You Are

You are their assignment. While you sleep, as you eat, on the job, on the plane, in the car, on the bus, and the train; they are there. You are their assignment until your assignment is fulfilled. Invisible, so many, assignments yes, they have plenty. God has given them charge over you. That's how special you are to God.

Encouragement: Hebrews 14:22 But ye are come unto mount Sion, and unto the city of the living God, the heavenly Jerusalem, and to an innumerable company of angels,

You are never alone. Hebrews 1:14 Are they not all ministering spirits, sent forth to minister for them who shall be heirs of salvation?

With all the billions of people on this planet, we hear about good and bad news. But what about the news that can't be seen or reported on live television. The news in spirit realm that will never be broadcasted how God's angels stopped things; and protected people from certain events and unusual situations.

Day 40

1 Samuel 30:6 And David was greatly distressed; for the people spake of stoning him, because the

soul of all the people was grieved, every man for his sons and for his daughters: but David encouraged himself in the Lord his God.

Find A Way

When all seem lost, find a way to encourage yourself. When people rise up against you, find a way to encourage yourself. When poverty tries to keep you down, find a way to encourage yourself. When enemies hate you, plot, and plan against you, find a way to encourage yourself. Find a way, find a way, scream Jesus' name and find a way. When suicide calls you, find a way to call out to God. Lift up your head and encourage yourself in the Lord. Find a way, find a way.

Encouragement: The Lord is your light and your salvation. He-Jesus is your encouragement and your Way.

David knew the pressure he was dealing with real and overwhelming. Friends had instantly turned into foes, and there was no on there to help him but he knew who he served. He God before he knew the men around him. He knew of God's strong hand of deliverance and his confidence rested in who he knew not what he felt. He got into God's presence for himself because he knew where his strength came from, he remembered the God who delivered him from the lion, the bear, and Goliath. You can't forget about past victories the same God who gave you those will give you this victory as well. Brothers and sisters in the faith find away and be encouraged in the Lord.

WHAT TO DO WHEN NO ONE ELSE ENCOURAGES

YOU
Journal & Reflection

In this part of the book, you can write down anything on your heart that you would like to remember during these 40 days. If you are fasting privately or corporately with your church and there are things that you thought about, prayed about, or maybe heard uplifting testimonies-write them down. Reflecting on God's goodness throughout your day is another way to stay encouraged. Thanking him for everything especially life and salvation. If you want o write a poem or a song just to God from your heart this is your private, intimate time with God. Maybe there is a scripture that stood out to you during the reading of this book, and you would like to go deeper in studying it and taking notes; this section is specifically for that. There are many days I've picked up a journal, scripture card, and past bible study notes that gave me another boost of encouragement in my heart and soul.

If you're in a prayer group or just on lunch break abroad and remotely I encourage you to write down the good things as well as the bad. Whatever things that are trying to frustrate you, steal your joy and peace find the scripture/scriptures that will help you to overcome. Say them out loud to yourself, repeatedly. Faith comes by hearing and hearing by the word of God (Romans 10:17). This is a way of meditating and getting the word rich in your spirit. All of this is intentional and done on purpose so that you can keep the victory, live in victory, and walk in victory. Be blessed of God in Jesus name.

_____
_____
_____
_____
_____
_____
_____

Contact Information

Kathryn Adams is an outreach minister at Solid Rock Holiness Church in Bennettsville South Carolina. In 2019 she achieved her masters' degree from

Newburgh Theological Seminary College in organizational leadership. Through the gospel of Jesus Christ, she ministers the word of God to both men and women incarcerated in the local detention facilities. She serves in her church administratively in whatever capacity is needed. Creatively God uses her to encourage many through writing inspirationally as well as teaching, and preaching the word of God.

Solid Rock Holiness Church 1004 Hamlet Highway
P O Box 1321
Bennettsville, SC 29512
Phone: (843) 535-5817
Email: kathryndenise124@gmail.com

Made in the USA
Columbia, SC
11 January 2025